A Day in the Life

RSPCA INSPECTOR

Carol Watson

W
FRANKLIN WATTS
LONDON • SYDNEY

Nayman is a RSPCA inspector.
His job is to protect animals from
cruelty. Nayman starts his day by ringing
into the office for information.

Next Nayman leaves home and drives off in the RSPCA van.
He is going to talk to his boss, Martin, about the first call of the day.

3

"I'm going to collect an abandoned dog,"
Nayman tells Martin. "She was fierce
yesterday, so I may need help with
a cage and the RSPCA ambulance."

Martin contacts Jimmy, the ambulance driver. He meets Nayman at the house where the dog was left to live outside on its own.

They lift out a cage for the dog.

Nayman peeps into the back garden. The dog is curled up in an open cage that Nayman left behind the day before.

"She's had puppies!" whispers Nayman.

Nayman protects himself by using
a special pole to pull the dog towards
the van. "Come on, old girl," he says.
"We'll take you somewhere warm."

7

The dog seems to know Nayman is
helping her. She goes quietly into
the cage. Jimmy and Nayman lift
her into the van.

One by one, Nayman carefully
puts the puppies into a box.
"There are four of them,"
he tells Jimmy.

9

Jimmy and Nayman take the dogs
to the nearest RSPCA Animal Home.
"Good girl," says Jimmy. "You'll
be all right now."

Nayman finds a quiet kennel
for the new arrivals. They snuggle
up together in the cosy blanket.
"There you are," he says.
"You've all got a home now."

Back in his van Nayman writes
down everything he has done
in his notebook. Then it's time
to make his next call.

A lady has found a snare round her cat's neck. Nayman examines it carefully.

He looks to see if there are any other snares nearby.

Next Nayman visits the RSPCA Clinic.
He talks to David, the vet in charge.
"How's Spud's leg after his
road accident?" he asks.

David shows
Nayman
some X-rays
of an injured
cat he had
brought in.

Then they
examine the
cat to see
if he is
improving.

15

Nayman found Martha, the duck, by the canal. She had been shot. "She's much better now," says David. "She'll be going to the Wildlife Sanctuary soon."

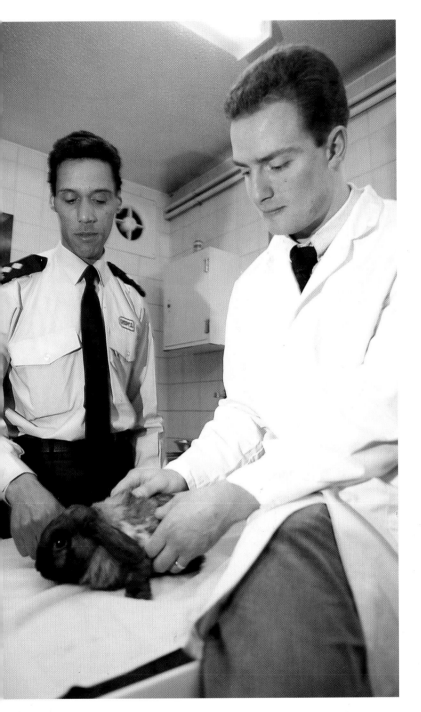

Floppity is a stray lop-eared rabbit. She is feeling very perky.

"There's nothing wrong with her," says David. "She just needs a good home."

Nayman's last visit is to another vet.
The vet signs a statement that will
help Nayman make sure that cruel
people are punished.

Nayman has finished his calls for
today, but he knows there will be
plenty more waiting for him tomorrow.
He goes home to his family.

Looking after animals

Pet animals need your time and care to keep well.
You can do all sorts of things to help them.

1. Always give your pet enough
   food and plenty of clean, fresh
   water every day. Make sure
   it has somewhere to run
   around and exercise.

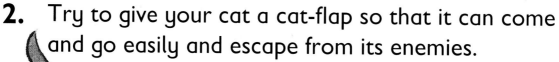

2. Try to give your cat a cat-flap so that it can come
   and go easily and escape from its enemies.

3. If you keep your pet in a cage make sure that the cage is large enough and clean it out regularly.

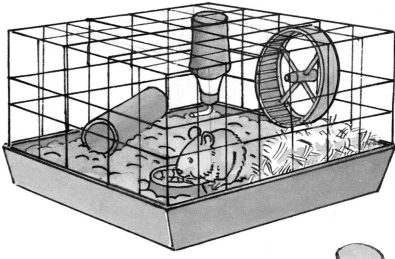

4. Always groom your pet, especially in spring and summer. Spend time stroking and talking to it.

5. Make sure your dog has a collar with your name and telephone number on it.

How you can help the RSPCA

1.   Only get a pet if you are prepared to look after it well every day for as long as it lives.

2.   If your family is going away for more than half a day, make sure someone is feeding and exercising your pet.

3.   Always take sick or injured animals to the vet, or contact the RSPCA.

4.   Litter and rubbish can hurt animals. Never drop litter and help to recycle glass and cans.

5.   Never throw stones at animals or try to trap them in any way.

6.   If you see someone cruelly treating an animal, ask an adult to ring the RSPCA.

Facts about the RSPCA

The letters RSPCA are short for the **Royal Society for the Prevention of Cruelty to Animals** which is the world's oldest and largest animal welfare organisation.

Every year the RSPCA deals with thousands of telephone calls from people reporting cruelty to animals.

The RSPCA has branches run by volunteers. They are responsible for clinics, homes and welfare centres.

The RSPCA also has wildlife hospitals, where vets treat all sorts of wild animals.

The RSPCA is a charity and relies on money given by supporters. If you would like to give money or want information on the work of the RSPCA, write to: RSPCA Enquiries Service, Causeway, Horsham, West Sussex, RH12 1HG,

or in Australia:

RSPCA Australia Inc, PO BOX E369, Queen Victoria Terrace, Canberra, ACT 2600.

Index

© 1996 Franklin Watts

Franklin Watts
96 Leonard Street
London
EC2A 4XD

Franklin Watts Australia
14 Mars Road
Lane Cove
NSW 2066

ISBN: 0 7496 2334 9 (hb)
0 7496 3621 1(pb)

Dewey Decimal Classification
Number: 361.7

10 9 8 7 6 5 4 3 2

A CIP catalogue record for
this book is available from the
British Library.

Printed in Malaysia

Editor: Sarah Ridley
Designer: Kirstie Billingham
Photographer: Chris Honeywell
Illustrations: Sean Wilkinson

With thanks to: Inspector
Dunderdale and family, Jimmy
Ratcliffe, Chief Inspector Martin
Marsh, RSPCA Dog's Home,
Oldham; David Yates, The Animal
Clinic, Salford; Charlotte Morrissy,
RSPCA Headquarters, Horsham.